Yorkshire Past

North Riding

Written and compiled by
Stephen Tyndale-Biscoe

at heart ♡ publications

YORKSHIRE POST

First published in 2007 by:
At Heart Ltd, 32 Stamford Street,
Altrincham, Cheshire, WA14 1EY
in conjunction with
Yorkshire Post Newspapers Ltd
PO Box 168, Wellington Street,
Leeds, LS1 1RF

ISBN: 978-1-84547-125-5

Printed and bound by Bell & Bain Ltd, Glasgow

The following pages feature a selection of photos from the *Yorkshire Post* picture archives capturing the character of North Yorkshire's towns and countryside, through the seasons and over the decades from the turn of the 20th century through to the early 1970s.

In some, it is the season itself which lends the picture its evocative essence, as in the image of Bridlington in the summer of 1951 and the extraordinary sight of the packed beach at Scarborough.

Further in the book Scarborough once again provides the setting for a wild autumnal storm, with plumes of spray rising high above Marine Drive. Pictures of York in the deep mid-winter capture the beauty that arrives with frost and snow. The photo of men digging a pass through a blocked road high in the Pennines at Tan Hill shows winter's other face - hard and bitter.

Some of these pictures convey the timeless quality of the Dales, and others can only be dated thanks to the cars on the streets or the clothing that people are wearing, as is seen in the evocative image of the Cleveland Hunt at Stokesely. And in the photo of Northallerton Market, taken on an August day in 1950, much of the period is given away by the clothes that people wore.

Many of the pictures feature images firmly reconciled to the past, such as that of the Humber paddle steamer, the *Lincoln Castle,* in the summer of 1960, before the Humber Bridge put paid to this picturesque, if slow and sometimes uncertain, method of crossing the estuary.

Sheep being herded through the streets of Skipton in the autumn of 1944 captured in our image recall a venerable practice which helped account for the town's economic success and regional importance. If it still happened on a regular basis, roads would be clogged with traffic for miles around.

Other local events are recalled in these sections such as the Thirsk railway crash in the summer of 1967 in which seven people lost their lives and 44 were injured; other events include the Harrogate rail crash of 1956 and the building of the controversial Fylingdales early warning radar installations in 1962.

We hope you enjoy our selection of images as they are a unique record of the life and times of North Yorkshire through changing times and changing seasons.

Written and compiled by Stephen Tyndale-Biscoe, 2007

Spring

● April 26, 1949. These splendidly ornate, Gothic style almshouses arose from tragedy. They were built by Elizabeth and Mary Isabella Gascoigne in 1844 in memory of their father Richard Gascoigne who had died the previous year, and their two elder brothers who had died in 1842. The designer was George Fowler Jones and the central tower displays the Gascoigne Coat-of-Arms. The eight dwellings were for retired tenants - four men and four women - of the Gascoigne Estate.

● A swift-flowing beck wastes no time dawdling among these hills as it hurries down to join the Wharfe. The trees are still in bud and yet the end of May 1973 is approaching.

● According to the *Topographical Dictionary of England* by Samuel Lewis published in 1831, the "township" of Airton near Malham contained 187 inhabitants and had a twist manufactory, and a free school with a small endowment. When this image was taken in early March 1955 it had a distinctly wintry look.

● A classic Dales scene with stout stone barn in a setting that makes the Dales so special.

● Pooled and as still as glass, the Wharfe lies beneath a thin spring mist on this May morning in 1958, the lounging trees on its bank waiting to burst into leaf.

• Whatever the year, whatever the season, Market Day is
Market Day. This is Bedale's Market Day, an opportunity to
view the wares on offer, to get those new shoes for Betty, to
catch up on the local gossip, and perhaps spend half an hour
over a glass of ale in one of the town's pubs. Many, alas, have
closed down since this picture was taken on April 13, 1954.

●This aerial view of Aysgarth Falls and their environs was captured on May 19, 1936. Here, near the village of Aysgarth, the River Ure cascades over a series of broad limestone steps, providing Wensleydale with one of its most famous beauty spots.

• No talk of floods caused by Global Warming when this picture was taken of a delivery truck barging past a marooned Ford Zodiac on the Guiseley to Burley in Wharfedale road on March 31, 1960. Floods then were simply put down to too much rain falling too quickly to be able to drain away.

● Pupils of Harrogate Grammar School "dig for victory" on their own allotments in this war-time scene which was being repeated up and down the country as civilians - young and old - put their backs into the war effort against the Nazis.

• Judging by the sight of these people cheerfully taking a dip in Ilkley's Lido Outdoor Swimming Pool on May 30, 1939, there must have been an exceptionally warm spell towards the end of May that year.

• A Jowett Javelin in Brook Street, Ilkley, seen from Wells Promenade looking down Brook Street on March 7, 1950. The Javelin was produced from 1947 to 1953 by Jowett of Bradford and designed by Gerald Palmer during World War II. It had a maximum speed of 77 mph, and 23,000 of these distinctive cars were built.

● Not exactly gridlock but May Bank Holiday visitors to Knaresborough were obliged to wait before crossing the busy A59 Harrogate Road.

● John Taylor does some ploughing at Melrose Farm, Bishop Monkton, near Ripon. Spring, 1960.

• May 15, 1947 was a Market Day in Ripon, the stalls
set out around the 300 year-old Obelisk where the
Hornblower sounds his horn at 9 o'clock every night.

• Robin Hoods Bay, April 2, 1956. Why Robin Hoods Bay? The name is a mystery, there being no evidence of a connection between this ancient fishing village and the outlaw of Sherwood Forest, or possibly Wakefield. It is more probable that the association is with a forest spirit known by that legendary name. In the 18th century, the village was home to the most active smuggling community on the Yorkshire coast. But smuggling gave way to fishing which peaked in the middle of the following century. There was also a thriving boat building industry too. After both these industries went into decline, tourism came to the rescue.

• Firemen and council workmen build a wall of sandbags as floodwater creeps towards shops and houses in Skipton on March 31, 1969.

Inspecting the lime trees following the public enquiry at Thirsk on May 19, 1969 are, left to right: Mr. W. Abbott, Mr. Hugh Nicholson (tree adviser to the Ministry of Housing); Mr. C. F. Walker, Mr. G. H. Rollinson, Mr. Stanley Rollinson (Ministry Inspectors); Mr. A. N. Leitch (tree man to the North Riding County Council) and Mr. R. Coates (the parish council's tree consultant). The trees were planted to commemorate Queen Victoria's Jubilee and have long excited concerns as to whether they should be lopped.

A sunny spring day and low tide in Whitby
Harbour at the close of the nineteenth century.

River scene below
Ouse Bridge taken
from the South Bank
on May 17, 1950.

The massive bulk of York Minster dominates its surroundings as it has done for centuries. In this photo, taken on April 12, 1947, Stonegate is in the foreground.

● April 1956. The altar, rood screen and Great East Window of York Minster. It is one of the largest areas of medieval stained glass in the world, being almost the size of a tennis court. Glazier John hornton made it between 1405-08 and it cost £58, a sum paid by the Bishop of Durham, Walter Skirlaw. For that amount of money in 1400, nearly 7,000 pairs of boots could have been bought.

• Her open foredeck packed with hardy souls, the *Bridlington Queen* powers out of Bridlington harbour on this day in May, 1948.

• This view of Stokesley, pictured in May 1950, shows off the town's large range of building styles, which include some fine examples of Georgian architecture. A milk churn stands beside the delivery lorry, precariously piled up with crates.

• Northallerton - its town hall, seen here on an April day in 1948 - first became an important market centre when it received its Royal Charter in 1200. Its regional status was confirmed when it provided the headquarters of the North Yorkshire County Council.

● In this amazing aerial photo of Redcar taken on Whitsun in 1947, the resort's extensive esplanade is bathed in glorious sunshine. A large crowd is gathered watching a show - perhaps Punch and Judy? Towards the left of the picture the King Edward VII Memorial Clock can be seen.

● Whit Bank Holiday weekend in 1945, and Scarborough's magnificent miniature train couldn't squeeze on another passenger.

● Mothers prams and smiling faces
on Market Day in Settle, March 29, 1960.

● It may be sunny, it may be a bank holiday and this is the beach, but the two gentlemen in the front right-hand corner of this picture are sticking to their ties and jackets. This is Whit Bank Holiday, 1966, and there doesn't look to be space to swing a spade on Scarborough's crowded shore.

Summer

• Some two decades after this picture was taken at Appletreewick in Wharfedale on June 19, 1959, the New Inn acquired a certain fame as the UK's first completely non-smoking pub, a rule imposed and rigorously enforced by its famously eccentric landlord, John Showers.

● Appletreewick pictured with Simon's Seat to the right, provides a striking view that exactly sums up the unique character of the Yorkshire Dales with its flowing lines and robust little communities sheltering where they might. Many walkers toil up to Simon's Seat for the spectacular views.

● A placid enough country scene taken near Boroughbidge in the summer of 1917, but in Flanders the Third Battle of Ypres - "Wipers" as the luckless Tommies knew it - was taking its bloody toll of young men sent to the Front from communities, large and small, throughout the land. And these men would some day soon be reading names they knew carved into the fresh-cut stone of their village war memorial.

• There was nothing majestic about one of the worst fires seen in Harrogate when flames and smoke engulfed the upper stories of the Majestic Hotel on June 20, 1924. The hotel's construction in 1900, and that of the Grand in 1903, had proclaimed Harrogate's national and international status as a spa town.

● This threshing scene on farmland near Bramham captured for posterity in this image would have seemed to those involved in the hot, sticky, itchy work, like a wonder of the modern, mechanised world. But how obsolete this reliance on muscle - both human and animal - would soon be rendered.

The Great Yorkshire Showground seen from the air in July 1969.

When a light engine collided with an empty horse box and a 40-ton passenger coach on the north side of Harrogate station on the night of August 7, 1956, the coach finished up at an angle of about 40 degrees with one corner in the unoccupied front room of a house and the other at the top of a 20ft high embankment.

Station Square, Harrogate, pictured during the First World War. To the right is the Queen Victoria Statue erected in 1887.

Spectators cast knowing eyes over the unfolding scene at the Great Yorkshire Show in the 1950s - and barely a woman among them.

● Harrogate's Royal Hall pictured at the turn of
the century when the town's reputation was being
established as one of Europe's leading spa resorts.

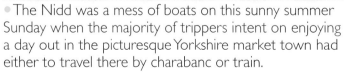

● The Nidd was a mess of boats on this sunny summer Sunday when the majority of trippers intent on enjoying a day out in the picturesque Yorkshire market town had either to travel there by charabanc or train.

• Punting on the Nidd in the shadow of the ruins of
Knaresborough Castle. Could anything be more placid?

• Car buffs will recognise the Ford Anglia with its raked rear window, the Ford Corsair and the famously unreliable rear-engined Hillman Imp parked on the square at the centre of Middleham. The year is 1970.

● Viewed in the summer of 1910 from the
grounds of Knaresborough Castle is the 90ft-high
and 338ft-long viaduct built in 1851 to carry
rail traffic across the Nidd Gorge. The scene has
changed remarkably little in the intervening years.

● Spectacularly, High Force on the Upper Teesdale Raby Estate, reputedly England's largest waterfall, plunges over the Whin Sill into a deep pool 69ft below.

● A picture of tranquility: this scene of the River Wharfe
in Otley was photographed on June 28, 1938.

● " I'm sure I had one." Perhaps the boy in short trousers was thinking this as he hunted though his pockets in search of an illusive sixpenny piece when this photo was taken on the Wednesday market day, High Street, Northallerton, August 16, 1950.

• Looking over the bridge towards the
High Street in Pateley Bridge, July 1953.

• All was hustle and bustle when this picture
was taken, in August 1947, of the market-
day scene in Otley. There is, perhaps, little
to indicate the post-war austerity, then at
its height. Indeed rationing would not end
until July 4, 1954 - 14 years after it had been
introduced in order to eke out dwindling
food supplies as the Nazi U-boat stranglehold
tightened on the shipping lanes curtailing vital
supplies to Britain.

• July 1955: a summer's day in the Dales - and you can practically smell the newly-mown hay. The field belongs to Porch House Farm - and although picturesque, a tractor such as this, providing no protection for its driver, was one of the most dangerous pieces of equipment on the land. Rolling over, they caused many fatalities.

● Richmond's bustling open air market, August 11, 1945. There are 57 "Richmonds" around the world, and this one in North Yorkshire is reputedly the original. The word derives from the Norman "Riche-Mont" meaning Strong Hill. In 1768 John Wesley preached in the market place and in 1771 the Old Market Cross was replaced by the present obelisk. It was originally built over a large reservoir, which supplied the townsfolk with drinking water.

● This stunning aerial view of Richmond was taken in the summer of 1953. Work on building Richmond Castle began in 1071 by Alan Rufus, a relation of William I. In the mid 12th century, Conan "The Little", Earl of Richmond and Duke of Brittany, added to the Great Keep, which was finished by Henry II. In 1174 King William of Scotland was held prisoner there.

August Bank Holiday at Robin Hoods Bay - and most unusually, it isn't raining.

Five men, looking decidedly damp, in a very large hole on the front in Royal Albert Drive early in the 20th century, Scarborough.

● Summer 1898 on Foreshore Road, Scarborough, and business is slack for the donkeys. Scarborough was then a resort of choice for the wealthy, but the upper classes seem not to be all that cheerful about being there.

● St. Nicholas Gardens, Scarborough, looking decidedly genteel on this gloriously sunny day in the summer of 1905.

Raincoat and hats on a wet summer's day in
Westborough, Scarborough. The car is a Rover
P460 and this image was taken in July 1962.

• Threshing machine dating from 1928 seen working at Burtree House, Hutton Sessay, near Thirsk, in August 1971.

Seven people died and 44 were injured when a London-Edinburgh express with 300 passengers aboard hit a derailed goods train near Thirsk in the summer of 1967.

Thorner Parish Church, framed by the bridge that carried the railway line from Church Fenton to Wetherby, photographed on June 3, 1960. The railway was closed under the Beeching plan, and the bridge was subsequently demolished. Following the Beeching report's publication in 1963, over 4,000 miles of railway and 3,000 stations were closed.

● August 5, 1976, Scarcroft Tollhouse, built after the construction of the Leeds/Wetherby road in 1826. Tolls continued to be levied for around 50 years until the road became a public highway.

Donkeys, beach chairs and bathing machines on Whitby Beach in the last decade of the 19th century. In the foreground, a foal is being introduced to the world where it will spend its working life.

• The beach at Bridlington North Side is packed and
the sand is dry on Thursday, August 9, 1951. But there
is not much evidence of the holidaymakers stripping
down to catch the sun. Rather the contrary in fact.

• Print frocks - well below the knee - shirts, jackets
and even a pair of braces were the casual wear to be
seen at Bolton Abbey on August Bank Holiday, 1955.

• The pleasure boats are filled, and the crowds throng Bridlington Harbour on June 21, 1951.

• Yorkshire cobbles drawn up along the front at Filey on this sunny August day in 1965.

● A young boy gazes at the paddle steamer *Lincoln Castle* steaming away from Hull Victoria Pier across the Humber to New Holland in the summer of 1960. She was built in 1940 and could carry cars - the top of one can just be seen towards her stern - as well as passengers. On arrival at New Holland they were able to catch a special train to Grimsby which reached the ferry via the 430-yard (400 meter) long pier. After the opening of the Humber Bridge in June 1981, the ferry was decommissioned. New Holland Pier was taken over by New Holland Bulk Services, and Hull Pier lost its pontoon. The *PS Lincoln Castle* eventually moved to Alexandra Dock in Grimsby, near the National Fishing Heritage Centre.

● A bathing belle poses by a yacht drawn up on to the beach of Runswick Bay on August 8, 1951. The bay provided safe anchorage for fishing boats for more than 600 years, and when the industry declined, its picturesque setting attracted first artists and then holidaymakers.

• Motorcycle racing in Scarborough, July 1955. The rider
on Number 33 would seem to be at a slight disadvantage,
having a pillion passenger on his machine.

• Three riders seem to have the beach at Sandsend to
themselves when this picture was taken on July 1, 1949.
Kettleness point can be seen in the background. This
photograph illustrates perfectly why the seaside village,
sitting at the foot of Lythe Bank, got its name.

• All set for a donkey derby on Scarborough's South Shore on this sunny August day in 1954. While some of these young riders might be eager for the "off", the donkeys look most unlikely to break into a trot, let alone a gallop.

• Market Day in Settle, the bustling Market Square dominated by the Shambles, a unique three-storey building with shops below and houses above.

Autumn

● Aldwark, near Boroughbridge, October 6, 1953. Barges passing beneath the toll bridge en route for York. Latterly Aldwark became home to a water activity and outdoor education centre owned and managed by Central Yorkshire Scout Council. For cyclists the chief delight is the quaint toll bridge which they can cross without paying.

● October, 1962. The Fylingdales early-warning "golf ball" radar installations were constructed despite vociferous local and national protests at what was seen to be a desecration of the North York Moors. But when they became redundant and were dismantled in August 1989 to be replaced by a truncated pyramid, there was another out-cry - this time on their behalf.

• Seen from the air, the Fylingdales "golf balls", which would become a landmark for those travelling on the A169 Pickering to Whitby road, or for walkers toiling across the North York Moors.

First Car To OTLEY. Sept 8th 1915. (2)

● An historic photo of the first tram car in Otley, taken on September 8, 1915.

● Middleham Church, as seen on September 18, 1967. Close by is Middleham's famous castle, the much-loved childhood home of Richard III. By the mid-15th century, the castle's owners, the powerful Neville family, had turned it into a fortified palace. Found near the castle was the Middleham Jewel, a 15th-century pendant decorated with a large sapphire.

The essence of an autumn day in Reeth, Swaledale, October 1954.

October 1959. Framed by the 18th century Obelisk and the Church of the Holy Trinity, coaches and buses line up in Richmond's cobbled Market Square, said to be one of the largest in England.

The narrow, winding lanes of Robin Hoods Bay are a feature of this old and picturesque fishing village which charms the visitors who go there. This scene was captured in September 1963.

• A flock of sheep being driven through the streets of Skipton on October 11, 1944, to the livestock market. The market had made the town an important wool trading centre - and there's plenty of wool being herded along here.

The brigade of Gurkhas band contingent appearing at York Tattoo play a selection of music in St. Helen's Square, York, on September 15 1971.

• Leyburn Market Place on September 9, 1950, where a queue of people waits for a bus. Friday markets have been held in Leyburn since the 17th century.

• Not a ripple disturbs the glassy surface at the moorings on the meandering River Ouse at Acaster Malbis on this still October day in 1956.

● A huge wave crashes into the side of Scarborough's exposed Marine Drive during an autumn storm in 1958, sending up a plume of spray as high as Nelson's Column.

● The same storm in 1958. It was definitely a big mistake to attempt driving along the front in these conditions. The car up to its axels looks to be in danger of being washed away - and there is a good crowd of people who will see it go. Some of these spectators are perhaps too close to that wild, unpredictable sea to be entirely safe.

• Mill stones lean up against the walls of the
250-year old mill at Spofforth on October 30,
1972, and a girl tentatively examines the bridge
that arches over the dry bed of the old mill race.

● Among shoppers hunting for something for the family in Stockton on Tees market on October 25, 1946, a group of boys find something of interest at a stall piled with an assortment of tubes and lengths of timber.

Winter

• The escarpment rising to the North York Moors provides a backdrop to the grand if austere buildings of Ampleforth College, the largest private Catholic boarding school in the country. It first opened in 1802 and is run by the Benedictine monks of Ampleforth Abbey. In 1974 its abbot, Basil Hume, was appointed Archbishop of Westminster and the de facto head of the Catholic Church in England and Wales.

● The cars on the roadside, a Ford Popular and a Morris Oxford, date this photo of the Craven Arms in Appletreewick, but little else has changed in the succeeding decades since that day in February 1958 when it was taken, suggesting a timeless quality for which the Dales are loved.

● A snowy lane near Arthington in January 1960, provides testing conditions even for a sure-footed Mini. The revolutionary little car - this one owned by Mr Geoff Halton - first hit the headlines just a year earlier in 1959.

The ancient church of St. Mary's, Askham Bryan, pictured here on February 1, 1954, dates from Norman times, but for many hundreds of years it was never warm enough inside to melt the snow that fell on its roof on a wintry day such as this.

• An archetypical village idyll on a still winter's day? Look more closely at Askham Richard's village green and duck pond, captured in November 1953, and the effects of post-war austerity can be seen in the general air of quiet dilapidation and neglect.

• The men operating this snow plough on the Leeds-Wetherby Road in January 1955 would have known that there was nothing more reliable to perform a heavy task in these treacherous and difficult conditions than a heavy horse. It might be slow, but it was just about unstoppable.

Aysgarth Falls, February 1,1945. A cold snap freezes the famous falls, creating an extraordinary ice sculpture.

● What better place to be on a crisp, sunny winter's day than walking through the sharp cold air, the snow crunching underfoot, towards Grinton in Swaledale. This evocative scene, with Carver Hill (1599 ft) on the skyline, was captured on February 8, 1950.

● The genteel scene in Harrogate's Winter Gardens captured by the camera in 1924. It might have been warm enough for the palm trees to survive in there, but the visitors have not shed their warm winter coats.

● Havoc caused at the caravan site at Old Bilton, Harrogate, by gales in February 1962.

A snowy day in March 1949 made a picture-postcard scene of Knaresborough's Victorian viaduct, with hoar frost dressing the trees in crystal, and snow whitening the ground.

Knaresborough's famous Dropping Well is festooned with icicles on this freezing January day in 1959.

An urban horror story, this one being part of the new Dundas Street shopping centre, Middlesbrough, showing some of the empty shops with an exercise in banality towering above them.

• The new Police Headquarters in Dunning Street, Middlesbrough, December 11, 1963, perfectly illustrates how badly the public authorities and the architects they employed in this era got things wrong. This monstrosity was deemed worthy of a Class 1 commendation in the Civic Trust awards scheme, but if the public had been consulted, the vote would no doubt have been to demolish it - preferably with high explosives - and start again.

• The famously cold winter of 1947 meant fun for some, and these skaters on the frozen River Wharfe at Otley were no doubt working hard enough to keep themselves warm.

● Looking west along the railway tracks from Otley Station on February 20, 1948. The ramp on the right is an aid to assembling goods trains, the wagons needing but a shove to send them trundling down to the desired spot.

● February 8, 1950, was evidently a bitterly cold day in
Reeth, Swaledale. This picture shows the market place
looking windswept and desolate.

● Where the Malton and Helmsley roads meet in Pickering,
photographed on January 17, 1947, and betraying little sign of
the extremely cold winter. The skyline is dominated by the spire
of the Parish Church of St. Peter and St. Paul, which has fine
examples of 15th century wall paintings down both sides of the
aisle - perhaps the finest in the country. They were uncovered
in the 19th century, having been hidden for a hundred or so
years beneath layers of plaster. Robert King, the surveyor who
planned Washington DC on a site chosen by George Washington, was born in Pickering in 1740, and he was buried there
after his death in 1817.

• Somewhere near here on the A66 Reeth-Brough Road,
perhaps buried beneath the snow, is the Tan Hill pub -
at some 536m (1732ft) above sea level, the highest pub in
England. This photo of men shoveling the snow to cut a
corridor, with a snow plough glimpsed in the distance, was
taken in January 1963.

February 2, 1948, Haw Beck, Skipton.

● Skipton's importance and growth date from 1204 when King John granted a charter allowing it to hold a market. Along the High Street leading to the Market Place, commerce developed and in its yards and workshops, people from outlying farms and villages could buy everything they needed. Here the High Street is seen on February 2, 1948, with the tower of Holy Trinity Church at the far end.

Market stalls in Skipton High Street in December
1964, with Holy Trinity Church in the background.

• A snowplough clearing the road to Thixendale on
January 16, 1960, is almost hidden by a wall of snow.

• April 9, 1935. Work in progress on the erection of the
roof timbers of Thornton-in-Lonsdale Church, near Ingleton,
which was destroyed by fire in February 1933.

● Looking across at Kings Staithe from Albion Wharf, February 1, 1954. In the floods of 2000, the river reached the windowsills of the buildings on the extreme left.

• Gathering speed, an LNER express train snakes out of York Station in February 1948.

● Shrouded in steam, locomotives give a good account of themselves on the junction and marshalling yards outside York Station on February 6, 1948.

● February 6, 1948, York City Station and porters load packages and parcels into the guard's van or more properly, the brake coach, while passengers make their way down the platform to find a suitable compartment.

● It will be cold out there off Flamborough, putting down lobster pots on this February day in 1961. Life has never been easy along this rugged coast.

● Well-groomed riders and equally well-groomed hunters gather in Stokesley on February 15, 1939, for an outing with the hounds of the Cleveland Hunt. It is a sight which some might have hoped would only ever now be seen in collections of archive photos, but all that has changed since the passing of the 2004 Hunting Act is that the cars, then bearing the names of British manufacturers, would now all have the names of foreign-owned ones.

• The joys of childhood. February 19, 1951, and a smiling quartet makes its way up Scarborough harbour's cobbled slipway on this chilly winter's day.

● Black, white and many shades of grey combine to make this wintry view of the Minster from Bootham Bar, looking across St. Leonard's Place, quite startling. February, 1956.